ballad of the breathless

ballad
of the
breathless

poems by emily graves

spout press
minneapolis, mn

Ballad of the Breathless
poems by
Emily Graves

ISBN # 0-9659443-8-7

credit where credit is due:
Some of these poems first appeared
in the following chapbooks and publications:
*In the Trunk of the Female; A Rare Occurance in Which We are Entirely Permeable;
Learning the Art of Motion; Thirsting for the Big Scrub; Remember the Absurdity
and the Monkeys of the Street; Fox Cry Review; Nature's Echoes;
A Definitive Guide to the Twin Cities.*

Front cover image from the painting "The Great Let Go" by Jessica Dickinson, 2003,
oil on limestone polymer on panel.

Title page image from the painting "Heartbeat Breathe the Light" by Jessica Dickinson, 2004,
oil on limestone polymer on panel.

Printed in the United States of America

Spout Press books are available to the trade
through Small Press Distribution
(www.spdbooks.org)

Published by Spout Press
po box 581067
Minneapolis, MN 55458-1067
www.spoutpress.org

"At night, when all is quiet and calm, do this alone: Breathe out so that your breath travels infinitely to the ends of the universe. Breathe in so that your breath reaches your one point and continues infinitely there. This is supreme ecstacy."

—Koichi Tohei

Contents

Learning The Art Of Motion

South Jefferson 3

to operate, pull pin 5

Supposedly What Happened 6

The sweet smell of lilies gently going to rot and how
it turned into something other than what it had always been 8

reparations for a fracture 10

El Salvador in the Summer 12

the thing that keeps it alive 14

i'm gonna figure out what makes the world i'm gonna make my own 16

Something Like a Eulogy 17

Learning the Art of Motion 18

Wings Of The Engine

The Natural Order of Things 23

sirocco 24

Suburbs in December 25

Lifeguard 26

Living the Dream 27

Nearly Missing 28

simple song 30

Tremble 31

Working for Sport 33

Group Effort for the Takeover of Elms and Other Varieties of Large Trees 35

Potential for Conversion 36

A Rare Moment In Which We Are Entirely Permeable

Converting Potential Into Energy At The Apartment On 4th Street Southeast 41

A Wolf Speaks 42

Everything You Need is in This Paper Bag 44

In 45

The Girl Wonder   46
Oh Wanda, Lady Artist   48
A Way to Hold Two Things Together   49
How to Get from There to Here   51
ode to the animal kingdom   53
Washington State, 1994   54

Thirsting For The Big Scrub

Survival of the Fittest   59
Confession   61
The Feast   62
A Blueprint for Calamity   64
fact of life is a fact of closeness   66
descent   67
The Conversation: Had On The Occasion That Cortez Was Separated
From The Others And Suffered To Travel Alone Finding, When He Did,
Miriam, Who Was Preparing For Great Things In The Woods.   68
Spying on the Queen of Spain   70
see that for which you are longing   71
digestion, that's the important thing, you move on or you die   72

This Wall Has Several Exits

green   77
Something About Richard   79
Tuesday Comes Unassumingly, Before I Know it is Happening   81
How to Avoid Pain   82
Infiltrate the Courtyard   83
Generous Night   84
this wall has several exits   85
Sanctuary   87
petition for my brother, my made-up vision of where he goes, what i want   89
the grey house thinks itself into your head   90

Learning the Art of Motion

South Jefferson

At the end of the block the Vietnamese family lived
across from a mannered lawn where a woman worked
days in short shorts plucking up scraps of leaves and twigs
from between short spikes of grass which pointed toward
the Vietnamese, their broken house sifting decades of dirt
down to the street, plastic taped over windows broken and pained,
announcing with the fervor of a roadside sign,
"This is 1975 and nothing will ever be the same again."

The other end of the block, sidewalk littered with
shimmering glass in front of the house where
the hippies crowded in, chanting earthly sighs upwards
where the pot smoke filtered through the
hanging plants, filling the room as they worked to stave
off change

Next to the alley, the Skokstads lived in a silent or
screaming house where scrawny children jumped
at little noises and mother was heavy with make-up
while daddy threw his hands and voice until the
swing set bent in anger and across the trembling
blades of grass, Onie and Al drank for the cash
hidden under the carpet and drank for the fig newtons
hidden in the cupboard and drank to the bruises
hidden on Onie's arms.

Two houses from the end where the hippies lived,
the Braatens prayed Holy Holy with their many
shifting kids, every move a manifesto, every deed

an act for God and their kids ate sugar cereal and
went rotten anyway while down the block the drug house
tilted toward all the neighbors' kids making plays for their
addictions or a crime of any sort and they finally
got the slender one, the albino walking by, whose pale
sharp hands, though mittened, shivered from the cold.

In the middle of this all we lived,
my mother the weather vane, spinning on top of the house
watching people moving violently, whipping
their lives against the lives around them, slithering
with nasty tricks while underneath
these swarming sidewalks small and hardy ants carried
off piles of leftovers, in curved and tidy rows.

to operate, pull pin

and this is how
rachel goes crazy:

she can't see right,
and everything speaks to her:
the lamppost, the table,
small gnomes at restaurants

and she is never calm.

there is nothing small enough
or big enough
or safe enough

and she furrows into her bed sheets yelling,
'at least give me dirt!'
and when she is covered with it
she takes to wearing a yarmulke
and declares herself the queen of anything.

rachel starts singing
songs about ducks.
she snorts pepsi and
asks, 'did i not pray enough?'

she contends that it is a rare event.
i contend that she is right.
that there are people
who are bewildered
who never go nuts.

Supposedly What Happened

Little kids in fatigues out cruising the nights
on stolen hot wheels,
stomachs pumped out proud and feeling strong like
shiny cockroach bugs
too hard to squash, too big to go near
while the dark hot neighborhood slams in not too gentle
and they pull over to stand behind a bush
where the tree limbs hang out
and the leaves wrinkle
not silently but not too loud and

Witness! Witness! the blaring cries and crazy bang
as the kids next door pour wood and beer into
a cement mixer abandoned in the night
and

Why not start a fire in the cement mixer?
Why not pile the wood in just to see it flame?
thought little cockroach kids who couldn't help thinking that

This was a ritual and
couldn't help worshipping
whatever it was the cement mixer held
as the solemn exercise took place.
They heard click click like a real-life movie
turning the night ride into a carnival
and like a quickened film rolling it was a posture, a stance,
a parallel universe just like the bug-eyed cockroach kids'
only prettier or dirtier or more violent.

They watched the smoldering cement mixer shake up the wood
and stay there cracking,
the barrel luminescent and holy
soaking up the atmosphere—

     —and space!
        thought the cockroach kids
    space! people make waste make people make things and
replace them with each other
      all bustling hustling whining and it's more than
          recreational math or numbers,
more than scattered equations!

   it's compiled into what becomes a lifetime
   diet of jumping jacks, an attempt to minimize
   and canonize every morning every day and—

—the night turned into
the jittery hours of caffeine wake-ups while
little kids in fatigues cruised home thinking
what am i oh what am i.

The sweet smell of lilies gently going to rot and how it turned into something other than what it had always been

Margaret first noticed the subtle shading of smell 22 years before
she knew it would become her and she would forget
it was there.
It begins by seeping into her clothes
surrounding her when she moves too quickly
becoming so strong she drops out
of the Ladies Aid and stops going to the cafe
and takes
to incessant bathing
covering herself with bath oils and perfumes.
It's inexplicable
she slid out of her mother's heaving body and lived
with the same sweet smell of lilies gently going to rot
no reason, simply fact.
Husband Bud smells like cigarettes
Daughter Bea like piano keys
Son David smells like prairie grass
and Margaret's changed the shade
of smells leaking from her pores, it isn't her.
At night she and Bud lay close together not touching.
Margaret wonders
when he'll notice
and what he'll do
about the smell.
Squeeze all life from it in a thorough way
harness his relentless understanding to
smother its baffling odor.
Weeks pass, Bud mounts
her with predictable rhythm and moves

like fractal geometry
irregular and constant without noticing
slowed down shadowed lack of movement beneath him.
Margaret sits days tight
against the back of the recliner
legs pushed unnaturally over the stuffed leg rest
hands sewing buttons on
eyes staring into the off
off white of the living room walls
lips clenched tightly
like a crunched and bloody Kleenex.
Around her body forms
the dank aura of fifteen days of rain
less than the forty it took
to drown the world under
Noah's Ark and Margaret is waterlogged
carrying the first half
of the world's greatest flood
in her body
from the days when the finger of God
came pointing out of the sky saying
"Go forth, Margaret, down across the land buried under
the water and bring with you
an ache in your belly, twelve hours of sleep
and the effortlessly rolling hills of a place
where the lilies twist freely among untended vines."
and Margaret fell
on her knees saying,
"Yes, God, Yes."

reparations for a fracture

i was flying on the momentous whiplash of winter and i met him
he noticed everything except what didn't matter and i was
surprised i could move him

my legs became mechanized springs, propelling me
forward! forward! and he was there, a frenzied machination
that i could not have imagined alone

hello! i said, the world is a lusty vagrant and i'm traveling on it,
we are a wire, sputtering, hitting metal everywhere,
making it spark

during all this, june rode by pumping at a furious pace and
july poured in on the lush pungency of a slithery heat wave
while august gathered up all the poignant green of summer
and held

       held

i breathed deeply, looked behind me and picked up everything
to give him like some sort of haphazard gift
i learned how to repair things with my ragged mind, turn
fractures into growth, seal bones together again,
fuse tendons to muscles and he watched me

it became autumn, a rushing array of window dressing displays;
i tried on everything, my mind couldn't stop spitting out
words but i kept thinking he listened, he listened

and then i read that the radius,
the mobile bone in the forearm
requires the most attention;
its freedom of movement and alignment
must be secured and it is happening!
one learns to extend an arm just so far and pulls it back,
the next day a bit further until full extension is reached
and the capacity for active movement is heightened
to what it never was before

El Salvador in the Summer

Ask my brother
if there is something about living
right there
on that sharp and urgent edge
ask him if it yields some sick relief
knowing you are always living
a day or night
that could swiftly end.

Think of him now
bundled through the window of a tiny mud room
and of his mother
silently groping for her sadness
in the heavy night of El Salvador.
El Salvador, where for me,
the nights were clear
likewise the days
likewise the moments sprinkling between

where José ran
struggling across the gaping countries which stood
in his way
picking bananas in Belize, hoeing in Mexico and standing up
to the rivers
to face them like a 13 year old Tarzan
with tires and ropes and skin exposed
and after that the screams of guards
the footsteps and the trucks.
Hiding took on new meaning;

there was success or death in the cave
with the snakes which curled, which he ate
and the cave which finally he left to get caught and
that's not enough;
think of snow and school and the garden he grew,
with a butcher knife and a spoon and two months later
the red hot chiles he ate raw and whole
leaning over the stove
sweating and crying and turning red.
A punishment?

A reminder of something he would never have
on this mild and stocky landscape, Minnesota,
where he finally fell far from the tree
in jail and scattered children and
here my brother has become what he never would have.
So that in El Salvador when I looked for his mother
among the women
all selling the same something
desperate, sad or crazy
I kept seeing him
hands out and offering,
again and again.

The Thing That Keeps It Alive

Jerilyn Weilan pulls up her knees,
hides in her beehive and lets it all go.
Either that or she hordes it,
holding it between her legs as
she peers out of two pink curls and
watches as the world turns
better than hers ever did and
mentally locks locks
locks all the doors in her house.

Dalen Weilan is tied to the swing out back
and his crew cut army dad
pushes him through the yard
like a metronome screaming,
"Don't be afraid, you goddamn pussy!"
Dalen just screams.

Glory and Jonna stand transfixed
by the train set in the basement and
get slapped like dough or ignored even harder.
Glory keeps repeating to herself,
"Metal melts exactly like wax, except hotter.
Metal melts exactly like wax, except hotter."
Jonna learns how to move an eyebrow.

Jerilyn Weilan hides in her beehive and
paints her eyes blue,
her nails pink and
her cheeks red.
She smokes and makes do
while her son swings screaming
her girls speak softly
and she lets the world go.

i'm gonna figure out what makes the world
i'm gonna make my own

watch as the crazy white sun
hits the glassy-eyed sky
its rattling progress over
the glittering edge of the broken mountains.

these are the old ones
counting a billion years
since they sprouted fire
and moved
blistering a parched level
between stream and crackling mountain.

but, if the sun were to move
to be shocked into color,
if the sky were to release and drain itself of grey
if the water began to rush, tumbling over edges
if it were to feed small sprouts in the cracks of the rocks
if they became enormous and proud, twining limbs to form land.

Something Like A Eulogy

You fell in love with an architect from New York.
You gave him your heart and he gave you his evening.
He had a lover at home and nothing to lose.

Against a brick wall, he kissed you madly.
It resolved stars and their movements, how they shift like crowds.
You hung hundreds of strings from your body to his.

After two days of panting, he left.
You count grass blades for hours and make piles of dust.
He had a lover at home and nothing to lose.
You are sparse in your language and thick in your gut.

You gave him your heart and he gave you his evening.
You hung hundreds of strings from your body to his.
After two days of panting, he left.

There were ten months of sadness, then you quit writing verse.
It resolved stars and their movements, how they shift like crowds.
You are sparse in your language and thick in your gut.

Learning the Art of Motion

In the chattering lilies of the garden
I remember
oh
having been quiet
having watched roots tangle downwards
towards the inside of the earth
slowly:

Whisper
if you can in the yellowish grass,
become the blinking unbeliever and
know that molecules
are like moths
gathering on a grid-like screen
vibrating wildly at a touch
and ready to open wide:

See that a wall is as porous as a screen and
if you know the air is moving as you walk through it,
learn the fervent action of your body
and soon the flutter of motion is everywhere
and you are surrounded by a boundless ovation.

Wings of the Engine

The Natural Order of Things

At 11 am in the blue-green leaves
there is a clump of black
a sudden ferris wheel of flustered flapping
and then the give-in to gravity,
to the outward pull of oceans.

Dogs, black-coated humans, break apart
into four zero-gravity spins
shiny quarters flipped into the air
leashes running, vibrating like electrified coils
in a plane engine, connecting who-knows-who;

And in a spastic, elastic second
the pitching and pandemonium stop.

In a head nod towards order
humans stand rigid and shivering
overcoats flung by winter breeze
and dogs run circles, snapping recklessly
at anything that can be gotten at
grass or sky, trees and leash, ankles,
the maddening stratosphere cry.

sirocco

outside in darkening september,
the wind scores your body like a sailing ship,
your skin gathering the skimming whoosh,
its insistent flight across your back.
the wakened bones rudder against the ardent swing of air.

a voyage wants trajectory.
i ask for ascent.

this is the small stuff:
that you allow a ship
to be carried away without flinching,
that its rocking doesn't harm you.

this is big:
your single sliding motion
you, winnowing
you, weathering the streaming waters
you, attending to the weight of matters.

Suburbs in December

In the fishbowl night the roads are full of moons,
clanking toy engines and the paw prints
of millions of household beasts.
Down every clean route are ant mounds, grub trails
and slippery winds moaning the night crow's caw.

The scene is set, spaced out doors
in grey rain array
shading the rows of unwreathed ill-fitting doors
concrete slabs and the blacktop marriage
of smooth tar and 4-wheel drive.
Like a mind blind with the tv humming,
the hooves of the dog's patting;
he's peeing on every signaling branch.

He squirms though fencing
under the brushing fir tree hand,
the normally unadventurous hound
riddled with sensible curiosity
and desperately looking for meaning on
the smooth lathed sidewalks spitting up glass and weeds.
He's already planning the region's next big explosion,
noting possibilities for redemption
within the regulation plastic siding
and swimming pools glazed with ice.

Lifeguard

Bob's gut hung over his swim trunks, an invitation announced.
When he did cannonballs off the high board, small children screamed his name.

I have never been close to drowning; more than fear, this is what counts.
Swimming can be formula, good etiquette and manners can be trained.

Accidents were couched in his clumsy trundle, the poolside slide and bounce.
He plunged into the covert deep end to break the water's smooth pane.

Did he take the small boys in his car, to his house?
The shit I cleaned from the locker room walls, was he to blame?

Water is made up of basic units, the lurching rush of pint and ounce.
People make use of its changing edge, make waves which could burst into flame.

To be held above the breathing line, there are lives I would renounce.
Bob drew it in like absolution, his lust for water a holy claim.
His gut hung over his swim trunks, an invitation announced.
Anything can materialize, anything can pounce.

Living the Dream

Outside the winter swathes itself around your dreams whenever you shut your eyes.
You dream in your open wood rooms amidst candles and books on the green bed.
Your eyes shut and flutter and dreaming, you turn the world white and small.

In the snow you push a peach around in concentric circles, a game of fox and goose.
The light is blue, it's low, your world is humming size.
In it, you fit comfortably everything that matters.

Your peach, its precious orange, its winsome fade to red, its green and minty leaf, serene.
The snow, its glacial shimmer, its fearless connection to the sky.

Nearly Missing

Leaping into the nighttime my cousin climbs the halo-ed trees
The rope swing wrapped around her shoulder like a shining lasso
A small pioneer, heading gallantly into the high branches
Yawning their cracking heave, shooting off into stars

From below, her spindly legs move like a rocking chair
Her trunk and small chest, bony and open, vibrato with sprite organs
And she climbs, her bare skin glowing at us from above
Her small laugh tinkling like a lit-up aquarium, blue, almost clear

And then, she does it.
She always does.
She drops from the top of the tree with the rope between her legs
Free-falling into the ravine
Rocketing like a pinball
An exhilarated bird, wing-clipped but finally free

The rope could snap, but it doesn't
From the darkness where we can't see
She squeals out at us grinning
The impish King David who leads us all
By love or by tricks, to her world:

Where the body pitches itself off limbs
Off rafters; off thin, precarious ledges
Up and up off of solid ground
Into the shriek of the forgiving darkness

To hit the water at full tilt
To land on boards lashed to swinging rope
To come settling heartily
Slammed into the earth laughing
With red in the cheeks and mouth.

simple song

The plane shivers across the sky like
your tongue across my shoulder blades.
You are so rarely afraid
and because you know my small self,
because you have crawled alongside
the whimpering sobs and held them
as though they would break your heart
too, because you have set off into my body
like a vagabond, with your small satchel
and bag of songs, because you leapt first
and then looked and then leapt again.

Tremble

I still miss the gentle hang of weight
From my shoulders when the small child
Hung on my back for hours and miles.
I sang and talked of things: stories
And facts i tested out on him and spun
Swinging him and threw him in the air
Fearless, happy and never dropped.
Walking home one afternoon, expansive
Tree on the corner fluttered in spring filled
With masses of returned birds whisking wings
Together and cooing. they rose up in busheling mass
Hovering little fluttered motes separated
By breezes mere feet above the empty limbs
And trilled independently, then dropped
Into branches again. the rise and fall
Drew us in and we stood there, baby
Long and silent, sea against my spine.
In the darkening blue, mormons approached in suits
Young boys learning the cool grace
Of predators, not knowing how to sense
The tender quelling of our street corner,
The baby, me and the tree of birds, asking
To talk, i told them in lowered voice to
"Say what you want but i'm staring up here
At the flutter and my baby won't listen
To chatter" and they talked, and talked,
Invited and enlightened; I tried to push them
From the fading scene.
Who couldn't recognize the clear window

Of the moment? when they opened their mouths again
My baby rose up singing the loud
La-la-la's of childhood, innocent and intentioned
And while they couldn't convert, every time
They spoke he rose up higher, singing louder,
Turning red, they walked off slowly
While we stood blending hushed
In with the changing blues
Of dusk to subtle nightsong.

Working for Sport

In the seasoned amber room
the orange glow pillows
your fly-away voice

the roll-around, the eyes shut
you read to me from Anna Karenina

the scene involving scythes, swathes
of straw, the yellow fields forge rows

your voice rounding out edges of
evening, blending into the sun setting

over the twin towers, my breath comes
in long swallows with the rhythm of rows

my mind filled with the steady pace
of the farming of the body, the room
groups itself into furrows, even swings

in the mellow dusk
and the russian peasants
after working four hours prepare to go
in to breakfast

we've been talking four hours
and i must prepare to go back

to work, but let me linger in
this moment a bit longer, let me

walk the wheat rows in your round
oh's and r's let me go again

into the gravel underneath the
cornmilk of your voice, in the pre-
breakfast fields half-sown,

to hold your hands
welcome in the daylight

start from the beginning,
the end beginning again.

Group Effort for the Takeover of Elms and Other Varieties of Large Trees

In the woods,
weevils chop off the leaders of trees
forcing the division to two angles—
someone must reach for the sun

and with bugs trembling in their face-forward leaves
trailing bumpy, eaten paths behind them,
grouping and going for the hard and calcified veins
waving and curling like burnt paper

the fulsome trees have a time of it
losing and producing oily reserves,
teenage girls in falling uniform
growing small and faking grins.

beetles send off the signal, to 'aggregate!'
and they do, worms rearing up
simultaneously,
one big group of mass defense
against ambitious low-flying birds
and mammal snouts.

sticks of trees remain after the love bite,
mountains of wingless wood
hands held up and blue panic lurching
leaving only the baubles
of yesterday's summertime girls;
frail things; pawed over and spent.

Potential for Conversion

The light cuts into the rocky clouds
behind the pub
behind the train
behind the block of council flats there are mountains.

You laugh, you stop and piss beneath the bridges
raise fingers to the steaming cars like engines
creaking across old tracks but
I am not fooled by your convincing tone saying,
"Scotland's not that close, this is Battersea,
no mountains here, you're thinking of some other country."

No, I am not fooled following the ripped pavement
up from the underpass beyond row houses
and roadmarks skidded in the tar
looking at the rich humps of candygrey
the himalayan kinks and whistles of skyscape
the reassuring sloops I know
everyone needs stretches of depending on rocks
of seeing them anchored in the sky:
this presentiment holds marriages together
stitched foreheads and the bass hum of two animal brains
piecing things together time and again.

The twin crescendo of crickety grasshoppers
finds you tripping towards the crispy cloud edges and
the grease and salt of England heaps up in dustbins behind you
truckloads of armor drive off to dark ages in other places
lit behind the hunched backs of mountains

accumulating cloudspots;
you can see it rising like bread dough
staring out at you in rows of sowed grain.
You can walk beyond Battersea without knowing dilemma
you can walk off singing boisterously
your best bar tunes
your coming attractions
roads to the moon.

A Rare Moment in Which We Are
Entirely Permeable

Converting Potential Into Energy At
The Apartment On 4th Street Southeast

In July of the summer I worked planting trees and watering things,
heat was the magic circle that swung around me like a hula hoop
keeping me awake during the day and heat was my conductor
waving me home again at night.

At home I laid on my bed locked into the white room,
my body running with sweat so that my hair filled with salt
and the air spun and dazed itself into seaweed and mulch for
the bed of my flailing imagination, harvesting mishap and adventure.

I saw myself from far above and I was sweltering into separate molecules
I was turning into pieces of breath to be breathed in moments of necessity.
I kept my room swathed in yellow to stay crazy and awake for my lover;
I was a warrior for companionship of the skin.

My lover turned up in the bustling glare of light and appeared to me in parts.
A flash of cheekbone, then a wink of shoulder and last, the bumping, headlong knees.
My bedroom began to fill with green and dirt and blooming color.
We rooted our bodies in the mud and grew amidst the stark confusion of white.

The building was bogged down in the sweaty jungle flinging itself
                                        out the third-story window.
Highway 35 stopped running and started screaming at my house instead.
The landlord's son threw a budweiser bottle filled with rocks through the window
and the lovely 8pm summer shadows finally crawled in through the naked light and
settled themselves around the apartment in quiet ones, instead of groups.

did i smile my small smile and break through laughing?
oh yes, oh yes, i did.

A Wolf Speaks

I branded the pounding rhythms of the earth on my forehead
and became the going in, the going out, the timing, perfect seconds at

        the interspersal interplay, the moose played tag with headlights
and chewed all the branches off trees

        the cat became the things i never noticed—a child for
the motherless who needed to love, a pacifier for the destitute

the sky took on an original flavor as the cacti turned southern arizona into a garden
        for the lonely, for the slow learner

        a cactus is wise and frugal
        a wolf is indestructible and hot as anything

couple with a wolf it is coupling with a living thing, the rage beneath its fur
        barely contained within
the moist plastic bag of skin which the heat keeps pushing at and inside

        small feelings navigate the inner ring of meat
        orbiting like bits of grapefruit in space
perfect pockets of juice form a fair of orchestrated responses
a small praying, the spray, the flying through the air!

she says, 'people are daily rejected who are by other people, who
       cares? we go on living, we still get fat, we move and if we're lucky,
                        we sometimes learn to speak.'

I am falling into stones, I am lucky, I wake up earlier every morning, there is a message
here, an ocean full of metaphor, a tiny song, a word that moves like gangbusters.

Everything You Need Is In This Paper Bag

I want a good god,
one with a sense of rhythm,
a god like an elvis collector plate
his sore muscles posing inside
the gold piping scrawled on its scalloped edges.

A small plastic smiling figure
to sit on my t.v.,
one that glows green from
the thick currents of electricity
pumped through his wire bones
pulsating with evangelical screams
and talk show hosts.

A god like a frying pan,
silvery edges throwing off sparks,
radiating navy reflections of
a kitchen curling inwards.

I want to hear the name 'god'
like the cat's fabulous meow,
I want to hear each raucous
letter drooling off the tongue
of a hot dancing honey like
G-A-W-D, like the howling from
a porch step, like saturday nights.

In

the hazy sugar sun morning sifting through venetian blinds in 1958 /
it is a woman somewhat like my mother/
(if my mother had sat down and not gotten up again) /
blue and grey like the side of a mountain /
strands of her greasy hair slithering down her cheeks like vines /
her eyes fried egg yolks like a dog with cataracts /
she is not crying so much; she's dribbling /
hands machines /knuckles clicking as she twists her fingers/
nails like metal / tearing afghans with her edges /
small smatterings of colored snow / spilling from her lap /
making patterns on the carpet / making rainbows in the light

The Girl Wonder

1. the girl-wonder plays violin

the girl-wonder struggles with the violin, it's bow has wrapped itself around her
fingers and tried to show her who's what and that's what's what
this bow ain't got NO time for girl-wonder and her wandering habits
always skipping lithely from one conquest to the next
the scratchy sounding of horse hair on metal is falling lightly to the corners of
the room, a small trip-trap of tiny cloven hooves and the STOMP STOMP of
girl-wonder's boots on the hardwood floor making permanent marks

she may as well write ENVY on the wall for anyone to see, just scrawl it up
there in humungous red letters, the girl-wonder feels ENVY for anyone with
fingers small enough to hold the bow and make it sing in a quavering arpeggio
which reaches all the way up to slap the ceiling flat-handed when all her huge
hands can do is spray a smattering of shot on the floor, break a couple of strings
and mess up the chin pad permanently

2. walking down the street

                                        is a process, a process, man
the girl-wonder takes the time to swagger, but, with only so much room, how
big can she be?
she hikes up her jeans like john wayne and all the people watch for entertainment

girl-wonder is a glacier, the glacier to end all glaciers, she carves a smooth valley
which she leaves in her wake and the people shift and shudder but they won't
fall down
her hair is knotted pushing
past her belly like the beanstalk it can be chopped but the giant won't tumble

3. plants

it is amazing the quantity and their distance, the space, the breathable air they
produce
she's got a million of 'em and more where that came from
she can submerge herself in leaves if necessary
it is possible to create a living home in green
forty vacillating walls of texture forty walls that wiggle around her body like
sound waves
it is an aural titillation for only the very brave with ears like empty pitchers
it is a vibration which endlessly wrinkles puddles

4 the mountain

she says, 'i've never seen anything so high' and then slowly opens up to
conceal every irregular bend of its face in her body
she rocks back and forth and croons gently
old country ballads sway from her mouth and hang loose in the air like the
multi-colored scarves of a practicing magician
the sun is momentarily silent while the moon waits solemnly for the final strain
opening night ends with an encore and a lucid stretch of sky
girl-wonder whispers, 'hush' and ceases moving for awhile

Oh Wanda, Lady Artist

At some dark-cornered party
you are laughing, bellied over,
slooped like a figure in a tiny painting,
circled around yourself.
Your fingers are curled like shadows
your eyes are cracked saucers
bloodshot from the force of effort
from the smell of paint.

"My poetry is in pieces," I say
"It used to move like myth, like magic and
now it is only chunks of static verse."

You take my small fingers in your smaller hand,
move them across knuckles and thick veins
through the valley of your wrist where
everything is fluid.

"Now you see, now you see," you say.
"I am a collection of houses,
I am a community of neighbors,
I am showing you how to build from nothing."

A Way to Hold Two Things Together

Week One In The Photo Lab

i lived for the close afternoons
in the darkroom and
the tricky passions i suffered in that red light,
my love throbbing against
the sound of water pouring
and the brush of the revolving door
etching its life through the warmth
and the warm holding her printing next to me.
i kept wondering if i should talk to her
what should i say?
how did i churn the verbal mess
that took off
like little breast-beating ants tromping into her heart?

Weeks Two, Three and Four in the Photo Lab

Her words formed out of rubberbands of letters
which stretched and popped into bouncing balls.
the room spilled into my world and drank it up,
her voice turning into branches of blue lights.
when she spoke, tiny green lizards darted out from her ankles
and basked in the heat and the words piled up
building a small house in my gut.

Weeks Five and Later

i let her live between my lungs.
when they expanded, she pushed them back.
when they contracted
she flung her arms into the space
and held them both in her hands.

Later

Etiquette in these matters is shaky;
your feelings of helplessness can be a great social asset.
while you should always say you've had a very good time,
it is best to let others take the lead in this giving business.
just think
how you might feel
if the whole situation were reversed.

How to Get From Here to There

The world reinvented itself
In the shape of a tree
A tree which became many
All wide and dark green
The color of late may
Stealthily creeping into june.
The trees pulled heavy to the ground
Their limbs filled thick with rainwater
I was filled thick with passion
For touching everything around me:
The grain of cement blocks
Clear grey on my skin
The rippled flesh
Of the tree bark behind it
My face flushed
Under the open-bodied look of the place
Where I stood.

The space above the parking lot was
A wide open window
The ground a sill I stood upon waving
"The empress needs no broom to fly
I am the empress queen!"
I was tilting back and forth
On the edge of the sill
With the tangled mass of trees
Growing huge behind me
The face of the expansive light
Looking out upon me too.

I was small
On the bottom
Of all that mass
But
My arms were spread
     My voice was smoke pouring out of my mouth
     Leading upwards in great streams of white which
     Were not furtive but bold.

ode to the animal kingdom

the wind is a blowfish
             the air a bed of dragonflies
             quivering with the enormous pattering of wings.

the caterpillar is still that lovely
                              stretcher
                                                          of skin
and even the inchworm is progressing.

I want to progress
with the smooth companionship of a tiger or lioness
where running is effortless and non-stop
and eating is passionate and necessary.

I want to learn the practiced stride of antelopes
                      the slither of the snake.
             the speculations of the spider monkey.

But, here I am,
How I stand in awe:
the stumbling surveyor of natural tasks
the half-blind admirer
the kneeled-down worshiper of tenuous worlds.

Washington State, 1994

Everywhere that summer there was the
scary expanse of hard blue sky
and there were no clouds for weeks
not one
just blue and the threat of fire.

And then we could not see the sky for the smoke
or the forest for the flying tress.
The jack pine seedlings were bursting that day
like kernels of popcorn.
The grey cotton of smoke filled us full for a week.
The soot gathered like coal fifty miles away
and at night we could smell burning.
All the skeletons of summer fell like bodies
and through it all
we solemnly sang for rain.
When it came it was crackling
against the dirt
like lightning.

For five minutes we were still,
watching.
And it stopped.

There was no warning
only the peaked mountains half tearing the sky
apart, what the rain couldn't do
in the face of all that orange:
it held itself committed

to praising the sun and the flames
which kept churning out acres
of shiny charred limbs
and we could not move
at the shock of seeing the rain bow down
as if the heat were more than it could bear.

Thirsting for the Big Scrub

Survival Of The Fittest

I'm starting over again and i like being free.
I'm a pack of ravenous, teasing dogs
learning about everything in a raging way
carousing to the engine drivel
in the backyard shed
where ten-ton trucks get fixed
every day so they drive like new again.

The rotting wooden walls
of the shed smell fiercely of yellow-orange sap.
The wood is spiny; I won't stroke it with my hand.
I'm continuing my lesson on patience.

There is a long freight train
piled with ferocious animals
spilling through the veins in my arms and legs
and a trick bear in my little finger's tip
helping out with crowd control
until I accidentally smash
my whole hand in the door of one of the trucks
and the fingers all dangle out
the other side of the window.

The trick bear grabs
the first ride out of my hand,
out of the shed
and heads,
wailing into
 the bursting milkpod of the night.

After I'm left, I stand
and in the shed all I want is to be clean.
Amongst the wood shavings and the metal scraps
I turn out all my jagged edges
and wait
       I'm waiting
       thirsting for the big scrub.

Confession

When I set out to hunt for something I wanted,
I picked up my torso like the hands of a plow.
There was a gathering of earth in my ribs.

How do I describe what it is to be full?

Imagine yourself in a shuddering bus.
You're flying across roads through the snow.
The light is like wool enclosing your mind.

How do you see yourself stopping?
Can you imagine your hesitation?

I couldn't have had luck every time;
my moment was a chance bit of litany.
I grabbed it and chomped at the bit.
I flung into the second by muscle group;
erectors following trapezius and hamstrings
as I pulled back my head with my shoulders,
flaring my nostrils and tongue.

I'll admit; i wanted possession;
I wanted some nuanced faith.
Take a look at my striated body—
From where does my longing plea stem?

The Feast

Inside the church there are women
you see them all
The steps to the parking lot
are dark
and in your white robe you are rippling
like ice cream

What do you care for these kind of vows?

The pillars of the church,
get perms and wave jobs for you
and families quiver like wires stretched from both ends of a bow

What are you waiting for?

The church is cool like cellars on the farms
like rows of jellies and canned corn you are patient
you are colored fruit shining through mason glass jars
there are glints about you so full they nearly ring

You have them
I don't know how
I don't know if you had them
one by one or if
they knew.
They knew

The secret society of lovers
a coven of women bigger than our town

whispered in the rooms of the church,
they spat out bittered nuts
and then they came unhinged,
the husbands left with ammunition
and what do you do with the pastor?

Oh speak of betrayal
the flock
lowing
the sheep
the breaking sheep

He knows of women who make difficult choices
who walk through deserts
still rooted to their men
no hope for the future;
he writes of the futures.

A Blueprint for Calamity

Amy works in a fabric store
when she's on break from bible college
and they teach her how to be
a good worker
a good wife
and
a child of god.

Amy lifts shipments using her legs
and carries them with her back.
She learns
how to measure and where to cut.
She learns how she can touch things and
how she should not.
It's the only time she's allowed.

She strokes a simple flannel.
Her fingers tingle;
she forbids it.
She slaps her cheeky hand
and feels a ripple down her lower back.
Oh Lord, her back.
She'd forgotten it and yet it had lived on, it had thrived;
grown muscles where they hadn't been before,
took on curves like a race-car drove hell-bent.
It reared like a surprised animal when she looked,
bellowed and craned its neck.
She surged for bolts of cloth
and the rows of patterns thrilled.

The pointed arch of the spine was radiant;
the shoulder blades spoke volumes.

Her spine's rotation impressed itself
in other peoples' minds;
they thought of it as a sign of something;
a blueprint for calamity
the way it snaked and twisted
when she grasped for far-off threads and snaps.

They stopped and said
her back made time move forward
it stirred up what should have been clear.

She wove her arms together and clutched her aching neck;
oh, the joy of being wicked,
the brunt of being right.

fact of life is a fact of closeness

he took small refuge in the heavy folds of her skin
where he could be warm and
just being warm is sometimes his one fundamental urge,
to lie with flesh pressed against his eyelids
corpulence flailing around him
like a weak and whining hull.

when he died she went crazy all the way
in the open eggshell apartment, smudged with the occasional
color of her racing cats and
the grime of the mess she stacked up around her as
if to roadblock the way out.
she went spinning off into the crazy fat world and
into his head.

say good-bye to the reclining silverfish,
good-bye to all the crumbs snoring through the cracks of the
wooden floorboards,
hello to the smiling warmth of a world before flesh
when he carried her lolling inside the swift curve of his hands,
when she was as weightless as a narrow and breaking twig.

descent

i'll tell you what it is like
to want to live in water.

it is a stopwatch in your forehead.
you are always thinking of the colored world.
your muscles want to work like fish eggs;
they shiver
and begin to move
in flat and lifting urges.
they want to shape themselves like currents.
they want to ripen into seas.

when you swim
you forget
when to use your breath.

the flip turns are what save you;
where nothing holds you up.
you tuck and cast your body through a high round space.

your eyes are roving, pulling in
the slickness of the glare,
the slightness and the tremor
of the breathing world.

The Conversation: Had On The Occasion That Cortez Was Separated From The Others And Suffered To Travel Alone Finding, When He Did, Miriam, Who Was Preparing For Great Things In The Woods.

Cortez looked and Miriam and declared, "I and my companions suffer
from a disease of the heart which can only be cured by gold."

Miriam replied, "I make baskets because baskets are what hold things."
She hooked her arms into the center of the straw without looking
and treated it like flesh.
She wove what was like flesh into majestic vessels.

Cortez stood by and looked on with shaking limbs.
He held his wrists to the light and could see his veins crawling with supplication.

Miriam's gentleness became a prayer
pointedly spinning at the great yawn of sky.
She surrounded her body with vessels.
She turned out her empty pockets and began to climb.

Cortez had a mind that snapped at opportunity.
When it saw Miriam take off into the sky his mind tilted and swung up.
It sent up bursts of begging flame.
When he wanted, he was nearly mad with it.

Miriam was sailing her dizzy prayer out of his leagues.

Cortez ran circles like a crazy hound.
"Ships which are empty make better time."
He knew it but wouldn't believe in it.

When he finally wrenched up courage to make his ascent,
Miriam had already dreamt up the bulrushes and rivers.
She'd already sent the baby along it.
She was looking ahead to a craggy ledge
which upon standing and seeing his dreams culminate
her mountainous brother would be carried away
in a fury of wheels and fire,
causing a rent in the sky.

Spying on the Queen of Spain

I watched the queen leave in the morning to avoid the wrath of the kingdom that had buried her crown, leaving her sightless and quite unenthroned.

The queen was dethroned and packed her bags and left on a ship, almost alone, sailing the atlantic and through the canals

with her hairnet
flying off her half-set hair and the hair itself set to the wind.

Like a battalion of long-winded generals, in the hull of the ship, she stood giving her last address 'cross the streaming ocean which carried her words like a bottle on currents

the mouth of the Marajo gathered and spit the snarl into the trees, hanging and oranging the moss, holding the sky near the river very firmly in place.

After months on the ship, after dreams of Spain, the queen's fine clothes began to fray:

yellowing petticoats, mountains of dust, and the filmy outer layers, flung into silky strands of former dresses winding into fodder

nesting the high-flying birds
that searched
for the strands ardently in the bays of the shore of the bubbling South Seas

until all of the queen flew across the world and became quite spread out
quite spread out, quite spread out indeed.

see that for which you are longing

i miss you
like i miss the cat
your yawning curl of spine
when you kicked
the brick
from the door with your foot
and we toppled to the bed
and broke it in the fray.

your knee pushed between my legs like a bookend
holding up all the ins and outs of me
while the traffic plowed by on the outside
gulping down the yards.

i unfurled new limbs and clutched with them.
you gave me a whole new set of attachments
and acted as my function.
you were my function.

you could have mapped new planets
with all the ink i shed for you
while you taught me words were my tricky friends
beauties to be toyed with and doubted.
i muscled my way up the tower of languages and dropped.

the end felt like a huge mudflat.
a wasteland of ripping and straining proportions.
the body should be more careful about its attachments.
the body should watch where it falls.

digestion, that's the important thing. you move on or you die.

a flower is blue, which does not make it small
still, it staggers and speaks of breathless things

we staggered ourselves accordingly and breathed
the ferocious flight of sparrow hawks

alaska is a sparrow hawk in the physical sense
the orange slash white of a bouncing universe

we place ourselves squarely in the center
of an un-square moment to click into place

the orange slash white in the physical sense
we work on cars for freedom's sake

for the sake of contentment we click into place
the flight of the bouncing universe

the flight of the universe does not make it small
still, it breathes and staggers and speaks of things

This Wall Has Several Exits

green

As summer neared and the evenings lengthened
we sat outside in those fat and hanging moments
when the sun is too heavy to do anything but
swing gently above the horizon;
a huge mound of incandescent fibers,
orangey from the heat.

The lawn is like a self-indulgent prostitute,
sensuously long and leaning back against
each blade behind it, the green made rich
by the late afternoons when the curtains
are shut tightly with only enough space
for the sighs to escape.

We are working our toes in the dirt
at the edge of the porch
making curlicues in the dust
telling fortunes by the curves of our tracks;
a pitcher of water sits between us.
He drinks from the pitcher
using the spout as a ledge
to prop up his thick lower lip
red, like it had been dyed by sweet berries
all this july.

Girls, like small and faded movie stars
loved to take that lip between their teeth
and bite down hard to try and taste him
loved to make the sun go down

and bite down hard to try and taste him
loved to make the sun go down
with the weight of their skinny thighs
pressed hard against the slats of the stairs
like it was the one small thing needed
to hold every detail in place.

Something About Richard

My father
reads evenings
Sartre, Wittgenstein and Foucault
his armchair turned
slightly away from
My mother
darning swift knots
pulling together the holes in her jeans.

My mother
remains rigid
straight-boned
and not unlike the inner workings
of a very complicated and expensive wristwatch
holding tightly
to my father's affair
finished fifteen years before
when he smiled widely and often.

My father
now and again will bake
loaves of rye bread as he did then.

My mother will still bite
thick chunks off the loaf
while it is too hot
eat them with her bare hands complimenting
my father's baking
and at first

when my father spoke with my mother
months after he met his lover
he spoke of him almost joyfully.

It was moments after this that
my mother began to feel a bit awkward
a bit wrong
about her curving hips and soft underarms.
She began to bite her nails and pull at her split ends.

My father stopped baking bread
and eventually
my father stopped seeing Richard and became sad
with my mother.

It seemed easier that way.
My mother feeling mistaken, slow and altogether unsure
and my father in love too much.
With Richard
With my mother
With the impression a body could make on his own.

Tuesday Comes Unassumingly, Before I Know it is Happening

I took the stairs of the blue moon living room slowly
in the quiet hour of carefully planted trees
and when waiting windows became too suffocating
I left and stood at the edge of the viscid darkness
watching for the moving hair of a boy
who picked me up on smooth and subtle nights
to take me places
that would force the line of my father's jaw
to become sharp enough to sting.

The boy spent nights not attacking me
allowing me my rolling tongue,
my raw language,
and my fresh sweat, bubbling like strength.
As a result, my unhewn smell
became strong in his nostrils
and the rough edges of his teeth
began sawing at every word
which was important to me
before Tuesday happened.

What he finally did was give me
a life like five sleepless weeks.
A violence for every seventh day
and spit which locked up
the corners of my jaw
with the fury of every
wanton move he made against me.

How to Avoid Pain

Imagine a far-off roaring, as of the sea.

Words like
"I don't love you anymore," become
the sounds of a car engine
starting up noisily in the deep winter
4 a.m. when all of us still sleep quietly.

The slam of a suitcase as she says
"I'm leaving," becomes
the sound of turkey roasting.

The "I'm sorry, I'm sorry, I'm sorry,"
the calls of seagulls over Lake Superior
two summers ago, sailboats in the harbor
rocks more blue than grey and

when she is gone you have heard nothing but
the sound of a car starting
the sound of turkey roasting
and seagulls
on a day too shiny to be anything other than blatantly awake,
not pushing itself into you, but, making you into what it is:
huge blue sky and
the open expanse of whatever
is directly in front of you.

Infiltrate the Courtyard

The days became sweet and tinged with
the solemnity of coming years
when everything would be
different and non-specific.

An apple would not be one
and words like 'comfort' and 'powerful'
could mean anything.

I woke up that morning in a lawnchair
striped like candy
and licking the day-old smell of parties
off my fingers, looked around:
"How odd," she said to me, "odd that
we are here
where we are and not someplace else when
we could be anyplace but here where we are."

It was then that we were kings and queens
excavating our crowns from the packed and dusty earth.

This was when 'powerful' meant 'red'
and an apple was firm-fleshed
smooth-skinned and round
such as the aberration of light around a planet
creates a circle,
a thin streak of gold which burns
even as it touches
the base of the skull
ever so slightly.

Generous Night

outside we are spinning cherries
from our fingers, turning around,
spinning quickly my brother falls
to the ground and there we are
the moon rising in the massive
elliptical sky the three of us
lying low looking upward
at everything incredulously
and all i can think is:
"every atom in my body is a star
every breath i take a billion years old
we are so small"
"so small"
my sister says and
and there is only to choose once
reach out gently and touch the hand;
open the quick pulse to the sharp air,
to the thick and mossy darkness
which becomes smaller every second
the world moves further past the sun
and toward the open and slightly dizzy moon.

this wall has several exits

the holy mama's thighs thick like slabs of ice cream in
the air smelling heavy of sulfur and per-fume just when

the thin boy with snaky spine stares through slats in the
wooden blinds out back to the shadowed summer lawn at

the slithery body of a woman with gills
slipping through the black water in a misplaced fountain and

the next morning under the green hum and buzz of shrubbery
the small girl stands at the bus stop waiting and just thinks
and thinks amid the screech and shine of traffic meanwhile

holy mama and the kids and pa are all in the wagon
her massive slabs of thighs spread
to smoosh into the scrinching air and
pa driving jolly but not fat
the kids all whining and tossing teasing snarls and
marianne getting ready to have her baby in my mind

all of them all twisted up
into a shady summer saturday feeling that lasts all day
with the skittery sun doing a number on my eyes and
the softly applauding trees circling up in the yard,
the south wind shooting through the screen and swirling around and
around and around me

and oh yeah, don't forget that i'm remembering

marianne whispering howls in back of me
giving birth to a thin shady buzzing
little gilled ice cream baby
that swims and swam and swum and swim

Sanctuary

Not the word,
but what it felt like
on early easter morning
dark wanderings of the night still sifting into
the early shadings of the day
and dawn was posed like a tiger
fiercely ready for the bounding race
from the fields outdoors
in through the stained glass windows of the church
for the dash up the aisle
to me

twelve years old and crouched alone
in the church near the choir loft
knowing that the ships of the world
could not hold all my bliss
at being here alone like this.

The sanctuary was draped
with the plaintive sighs of the altar
before the cars pulled in and
the peaked roof shuddered
with the rest and the yawn
before the trumpets spewed hymns.
The lilies bobbed and shied towards me
grasping at their last chance
to wind into voluptuous throes
a tumultuous cascade around me.

I was a small piece of the scene
but replete and redolent
in the heavy shifting light.
The dust particles in the air
were as big as i.

petition for my brother,
my made-up vision of where he goes,
what i want

my brother,
the whites of your eyes absorb the pinkish half-light of dusk.
you're standing on the inside of a grapefruit.
you're alone in a pore of juice
pushing your hands at its elastic edges.

where do you go when you go?

i look at you and your mind is a tangled prairie.
the grasses are drum whisks
scratching their gentle thrum before the terse crescendo.

would i be right to see you entering a marshy dusk?

you're dying polluted sunsets onto your face.
you're encased in the sweet steam rising off the heavy water.
you bury yourself in thousands of thin blue waves and i wonder
how often do you think of filling your precious lungs?

my brother of sadness
my brother of heart
i want to give you a pear tree for your dark side.
i want to give you the map to your mysterious gulleys and water.
i want to give you riverbeds to fill.
i want to hold you while you do it.

the grey house thinks itself into your head

i see you eight years old and standing on a classroom desk;
it's a thin chunk of rock poking out of a lake.
you're a fir tree, trying to grow;
trying to sway the class with your knocking quaver,
keening your account of the grey house,
the grey house,
the invasion of thoughts uninvited in your head.
after this, anything could think itself into your brain without asking.

i see you in your crying whisper
near the damp and hazy bushes
the meltdown of tar
in the old lady's driveway.
she takes you in and gives you milk,
it coats some part of you; you might think you're fine, but,
the grey house stings again;
it's nothing! a picture,
someone else's refuge
a soft dress of color
a kiss!

i see you run, your mind an entrance for random universal thoughts like darts,
like bees, like hummingbirds at a feeder, your mind is sweetwater for the grey
house, draining.
you can't sleep,
you're learning every detail,
filling them with significance.
your father finds you quaking and your explanation quivers.
the whole thing is crumbling

into a hum of notes
on the bland and shedding field
of your over-time mind—
this cryptic flashing moment is the don't walk or walk, the yellow light of decision
the groundwork on which all memory will be laid—

you taste canned peas in your mouth,
you're forcing down fistfuls of vegetables,
swallowing mouthfuls of oranges, greens and yellow against the grey—
you throw yourself backward and say, 'this is my mission!'

you walked the fringe,
the edge of the table,
you learned how to balance on string.
the outcome is that you're strange and
humbled but silent about it,
tell me: what latitudes and longitudes could navigate that space?

you settle for the light, the wind and voluminous hands.
you learn how to speak from scratch.